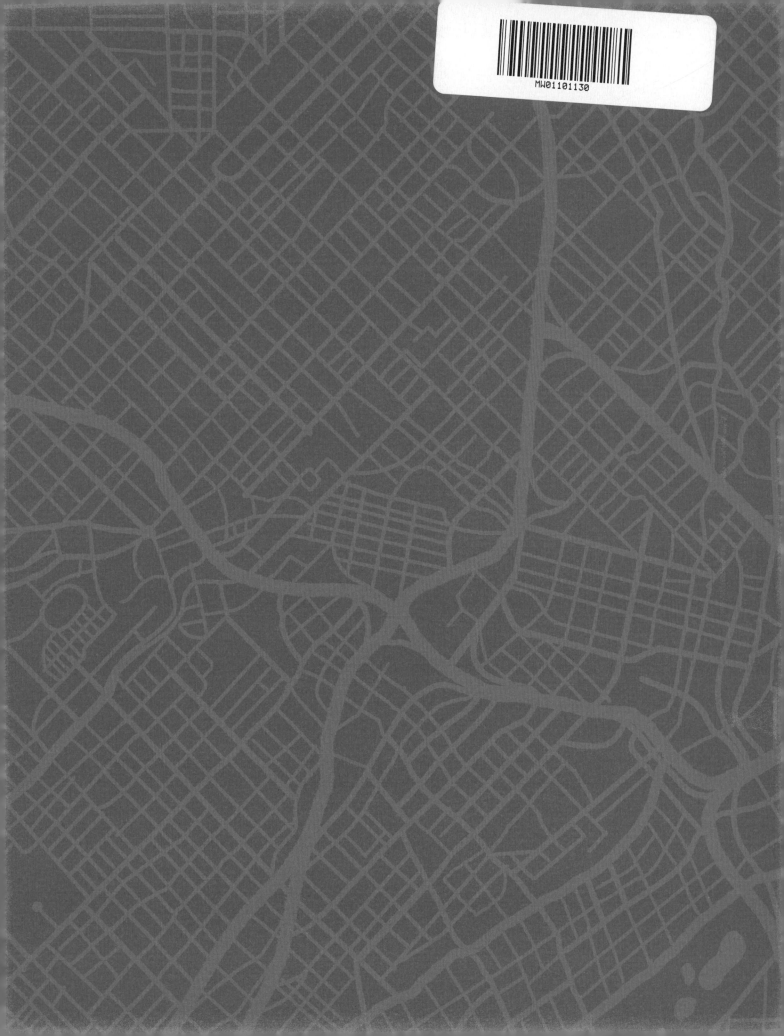

ARE WE THERE YET?

HOW HUMANS FIND THEIR WAY

MARIA
BIRMINGHAM

Illustrated by
DREW SHANNON

ORCA BOOK PUBLISHERS

Published in Canada and the United States in 2023 by Orca Book Publishers.
orcabook.com

Library and Archives Canada Cataloguing in Publication
Title: Are we there yet? : how humans find their way / Maria Birmingham ; illustrated by Drew Shannon.
Names: Birmingham, Maria, author. | Shannon, Drew, 1988- illustrator.
Series: Orca timelines ; 4.
Description: Series statement: Orca timeline ; 4 | Includes bibliographical references and index.
Identifiers: Canadiana (print) 20220436320 | Canadiana (ebook) 20220436347 |
ISBN 9781459835207 (hardcover) | ISBN 9781459835214 (PDF) | ISBN 9781459835221 (EPUB)
Subjects: LCSH: Travel—History—Juvenile literature. | LCSH: Navigation—History—Juvenile literature. |
LCSH: Transportation—History—Juvenile literature.
Classification: LCC G156 .B57 2023 | DDC j910.9—dc23

Library of Congress Control Number: 2022947180

Summary: Part of the nonfiction Orca Timeline series for middle-grade readers, this illustrated book examines how humans have navigated the world over time.

Orca Book Publishers is committed to reducing the consumption of nonrenewable resources in the production of our books. We make every effort to use materials that support a sustainable future.

Orca Book Publishers gratefully acknowledges the support for its publishing programs provided by the following agencies: the Government of Canada, the Canada Council for the Arts and the Province of British Columbia through the BC Arts Council and the Book Publishing Tax Credit.

Cover and interior artwork by Drew Shannon
Design by Rachel Page
Edited by Kirstie Hudson
Author photo by Grace McDonald

Printed and bound in South Korea.

26 25 24 23 • 1 2 3 4

For Mary Beth Leatherdale,
who started me on my book-writing journey.
With gratitude.

Contents

FROM HERE TO THERE

How many places have you gone today? Or this week? Or this month? Probably plenty—from school to a friend's house to the skate park to the store. Like you, our earliest ancestors were always on the go, finding their way from point A to point B. At first humans didn't need to travel farther than where they could find food, water and some form of shelter. So we'd set out on foot to no place in particular, just somewhere past the forest or over the nearest mountain. As time passed, humans began to set off on bigger adventures. We traveled for all kinds of reasons—to move to a new place, trade goods with others or simply because our *curiosity* got us wondering what might be out there. And all this travel changed the world and how human history unfolded.

The word *travel* was first used in the 1300s. It comes from the French word *travail*, which means "work." And travel at the time *was* challenging. Even so, humans were certainly traveling much earlier than then. In fact, if we go way back and check in on our early ancestors—the first *Homo sapiens*—we'll find they were traveling long distances. Most scientists believe these early humans lived in one spot, in what is now known as eastern Africa,

beginning around 300,000 years ago. And then, around 80,000 years ago, large groups of these humans began to *migrate*, or move, out of Africa. It's thought they first traveled to present-day Asia and Europe, later spreading out to all corners of the world, including North and South America.

Just why did our earliest ancestors start to leave Africa in search of other places? That's a tough question to answer for sure. But some experts think they may have migrated because of a change in the climate. They suggest a severe drought in Africa all those years ago led to starvation, and humans were threatened with *extinction*. To survive, our ancestors began to trek out of Africa to areas where food was more plentiful.

At that time, humans had only one way to get around—by foot. And we relied on the brain's ability to map the world around us to move about. As humans evolved, so did the ways we traveled—no more relying only on our own two feet. At first we turned to larger animals, like horses, to help us out. Then we took to the water, paddling to where we wanted to go. With the invention of the wheel, our ability to get around really got rolling. And once we'd managed to travel on land and sea, we looked up and worked on finding a way to move through the sky. Today we're looking beyond the blue to the reaches of outer space.

So how did we go from traveling by foot to blasting into *orbit*? And why are we so antsy to leave one spot to get to another that we don't know? Settle in for a wild trip to see how humans will try just about anything to get from here to there.

We have liftoff! Rocket ships may one day become a go-to method of transportation for tourists taking space vacations.

BORIS SV/GETTY IMAGES

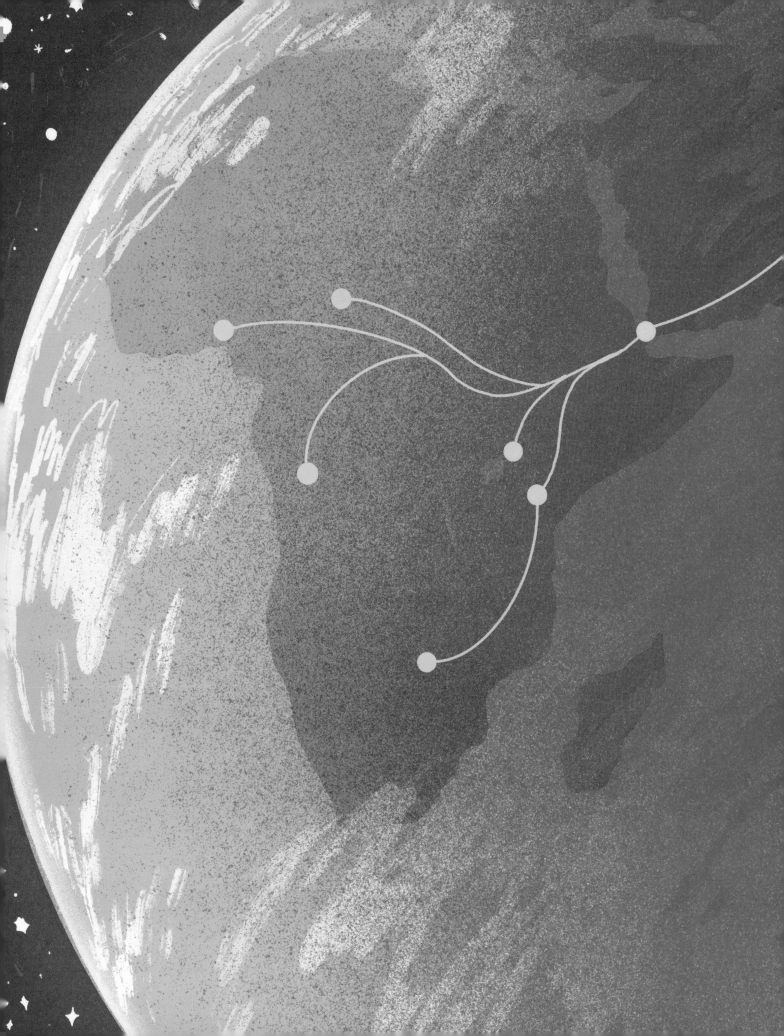

London cab driver tests
1865

Polynesian star maps
c. 1000 BCE

Australian songlines
c. 60,000 BCE

Viking animal guides
c. 800

One

THE BRAIN LEADS THE WAY

Sahara Desert sand dunes
c. 300

Have you ever thought about how you find your way through the world? Consider this: you can get yourself from your kitchen to your bedroom in a snap. You likely don't think twice about making your way from the front doors of your school to your classroom. You can probably even get yourself to a friend's house and back home again. Chances are, you navigate all these *routes* with little thought. And there's a reason for this. The human brain is wired to help you get around.

It's All in Your Head

Your brain creates maps so you can find your way through the world. Even if something gets in the way of your regular route—like, say, a blocked hallway—your brain adjusts and helps you out. So what's going on in that noggin of yours? Neurologists—experts who study the brain and nervous system—have found there are specific nerve cells, or neurons, that are used for navigating the world. While these cells develop over time, we're likely born with some sense of direction thanks to them.

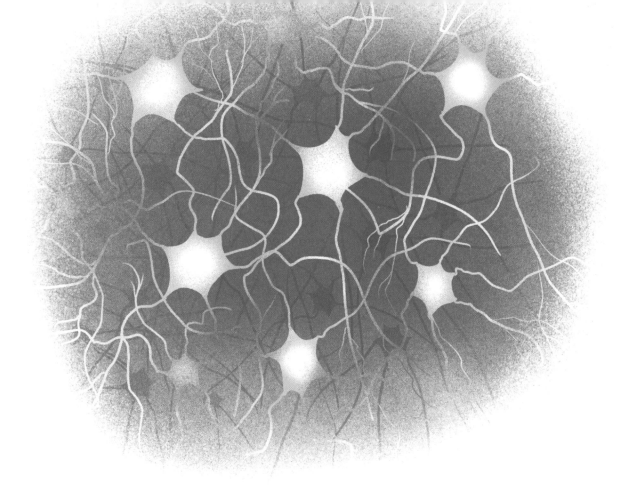

YOU ARE HERE

Search-and-rescue specialists say that most people who get lost tend to panic and make bad decisions, like running or ignoring landmarks around them. And after getting lost, they may avoid visiting places that look similar to where they lost their way—for instance, a dense forest—because it reminds them of the fear they felt at the time.

WE'RE HERE TO HELP

There are several types of cells in that brain of yours that help you get around:

- Head direction cells: These neurons are found in several regions of the brain. They help you figure out what direction you're facing.
- Place cells: These cells are found in your hippocampus, a region in your brain that helps with *navigation*. They are used to form mental maps. These are maps you create in your brain to figure out your location. For instance, you may create a mental map when thinking about where your home is in your neighborhood. You'll notice *landmarks* nearby, like certain buildings or street signs. And you'll note where they are in relation to each other to identify where you are. Whenever you think about the details of a particular place or picture how to get somewhere, you're using a mental map.

- Grid cells: These cells are found in another area of the brain that's connected to the hippocampus. They judge distance as you're moving about. The cells tell you where you are right now, comparing it to where you started. This helps you find your way around unfamiliar places. Grid cells work with place cells to form mental maps.

Uh-Oh, I'm Lost

So here's a question. If we have all these snazzy nerve cells in our brains to help us find our way, why do some of us get lost more than others do? That is, why do some of us have a bad sense of direction? Sometimes it's as simple as not paying attention as you move about in the world. One wrong turn and, bam—you're utterly lost. But it may also be that some people aren't as skilled at creating mental maps as those who are good at navigating the world. Why is this? Recent research suggests that some people naturally have neurons with weak communication skills. And these weaker signals may affect how well a person is able to navigate.

HEY, TAXI—BRING ON THE BIGGER BRAINS!

One group of people that doesn't worry about getting lost are the taxi drivers of London, England. In fact, studies show that these drivers have a superior sense of direction. That's likely because they have to spend up to four years training to get a license to drive a taxi. During that time they must memorize about 25,000 streets and 320 routes in London, as well as thousands of tourist attractions around the city. Then they take an intense test called The Knowledge, which they have to pass in order to snag their license.

Neuroscientists conducted studies of these cab drivers and found they had better memory than the average person. The experts even examined the brains of some cabbies using magnetic resonance imaging (MRI), a procedure that produces detailed images of the brain. And they discovered that each taxi driver who had passed The Knowledge had an enlarged hippocampus. According to the experts, the cabbies had used their navigational skills so much that it had caused a part of their brains to grow over time! And that helped their stellar memory.

YOU ARE HERE

Finding your way by observing the stars is known as *celestial navigation*. One of the stars that helps us plot our course is the North Star, or Polaris. In the Northern Hemisphere, Polaris is always located in the north throughout the night. Once you spot it, you'll know which way is north. To locate Polaris, look for the Little Dipper (seven of the stars of the constellation known as Ursa Minor). Polaris is at the tip of the handle.

Taxi! In London, England, about 300,000 cab trips are made each day.
KYPROS/GETTY IMAGES

Right This Way

Some people never develop the ability to form mental maps of their surroundings, so they constantly get lost in familiar places. They may even get lost inside their own homes! This condition is called *developmental topographical disorientation*, or DTD for short. Neuroscientist Dr. Giuseppe Iaria discovered the first case of DTD in 2009. Now people are diagnosed with the condition every day. Sometimes kids with DTD can be taught how to make mental maps and overcome the condition. But it's nearly impossible for adults to reverse DTD, and getting lost is something they'll always have to deal with.

We'll Find You

Could there come a day when we won't have to worry about getting lost at all? Maybe. A few companies are working on a technology to help track down lost people. They're considering a microchip implant that'd be inserted underneath the skin so a person could be tracked in real time. Think of this microchip like the one a vet places under the skin of your pet, which contains the animal's ID in case it gets lost. But this chip would be a tracker using the ***Global Positioning System (GPS)***, a navigation technology that can detect the location of something (or, in this case, someone) anywhere on earth. You'd connect to the microchip using a smartphone, and it would tell you a person's location almost instantly.

Of course, there are a few issues with this technology. For one, making a tracker small enough to implant under a person's skin is a challenge. And then there's the fact that a microchip needs a constant power source, and batteries only last so long. Plus, there's the big issue of privacy. Finding a person if they're lost is one thing. But do we really want someone to have the ability to track us down whenever they want and wherever we are? Doesn't everyone deserve some amount of freedom and privacy as they live their lives? As it stands, these microchips won't be finding a way under our skin anytime soon—if ever. So it's a good thing we've come up with other strategies to keep from getting lost.

Viking ships had the ability to navigate shallow waters. This meant they didn't need to dock in a harbor. They could land on beaches and riverbanks too.
VLASTAS/GETTY IMAGES

NAVIGATING BY NATURE

Our ancestors relied on their sense of direction to get around as well. But they also learned to find other ways to travel, even looking to nature—waves, the stars and animals. Here's how a few cultures found their way:

c. 60,000 BCE

Indigenous communities in Australia, including the Yolngu, traced their long journeys using songlines. These ancient songs are based on the land. Each one refers to a variety of landmarks along a route, like a curve in a river, a hill or a rock formation. The Indigenous people sang these songlines as they walked, and this helped them keep track of where to walk next. Besides being a way to navigate the continent, songlines told sacred stories about the ancestors, the landscape and the relationship that Indigenous people have with the land. These stories continue to be passed on from *generation* to generation. And in some places, including remote areas of central and northwestern Australia, Indigenous communities still use songlines for navigation.

c. 1000 BCE

Ancient Polynesians lived on a large group of islands in the central Pacific Ocean, including around Hawaii and New Zealand. They spent much of their time navigating the ocean in search of undiscovered islands. That meant they lived aboard their boats for weeks at a time. They were experts at using the stars to mark their position in the open ocean and find their way between islands. The ancient Polynesians looked to the night sky for certain constellations—groups of stars that form a pattern when viewed from Earth. The location of these stars helped them determine the direction they were headed. On hazy nights the sailors paid attention to the ocean waves instead. By taking note of the direction the waves were flowing, the Polynesians could figure out their position in the sea.

c. 300

The Tuareg people have lived in the vast Sahara Desert for centuries. To navigate through the desert, they pay close attention to the shifting shapes of particular sand dunes, recognizing them as landmarks in the same way we might spot a familiar building when we're out for a walk. They follow these dunes to find their way, as well as relying on the sun and wind to guide them.

c. 800–1100

The Vikings were warriors who lived around northern Europe and spent much of their lives at sea in search of new lands and treasure. They didn't have compasses, maps or many navigational tools, so they often looked to animals to figure out where they were. On a foggy day, for instance, they'd listen for the sound of screeching birds. That told them they were getting close to land. A bird with a beakful of fish was likely heading toward land, so they could sail that direction too. The Vikings also kept an eye out for orca whales. Since they were familiar with the sea, the Vikings knew where whales were usually found. When they came across them, it helped them figure out where they were.

Right This Way

Take note of these tips to avoid getting lost:

- As you move about, pay attention to landmarks around you—such as trees, a statue or a particular building—to get a sense of where you are.
- Snap photos of these landmarks on a smartphone as you go. This will create a virtual map you can use if you get off course.
- Stop and look behind you to take note of where you're coming from and what it looks like.
- Retrace your steps. That way you can get back to where you started.
- While making your way around a new place, follow your route using a map on a smartphone or a compass app.
- When in doubt, ask for directions.

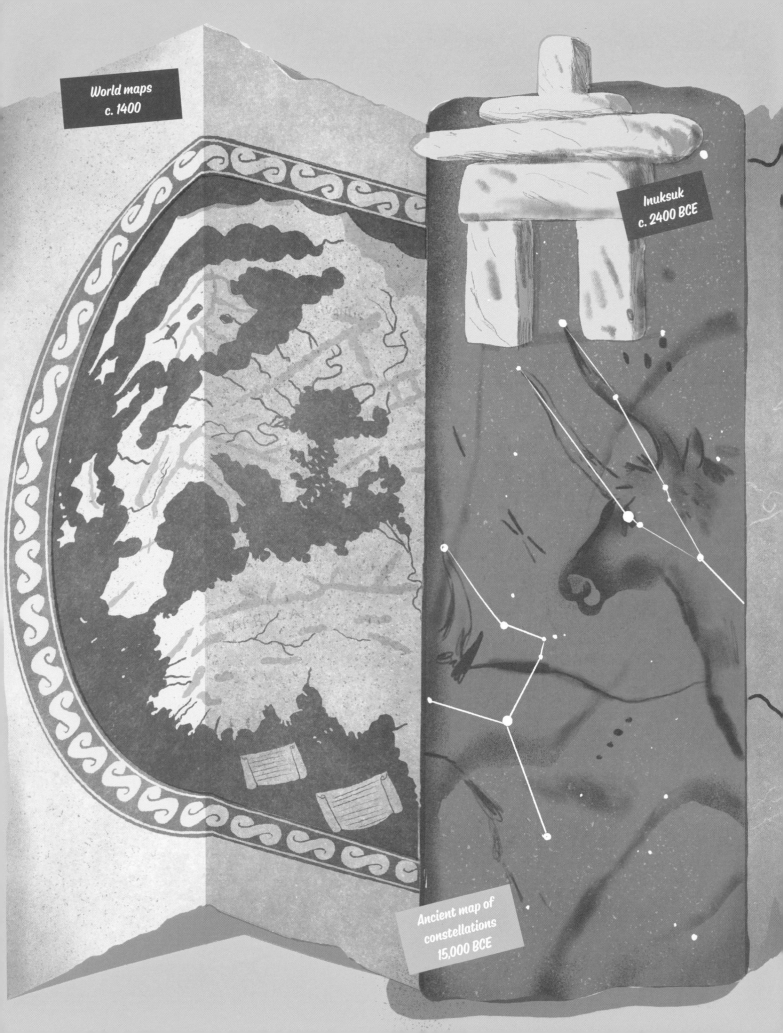

World maps
c. 1400

Inuksuk
c. 2400 BCE

Ancient map of
constellations
15,000 BCE

Two

MAPPING IT OUT

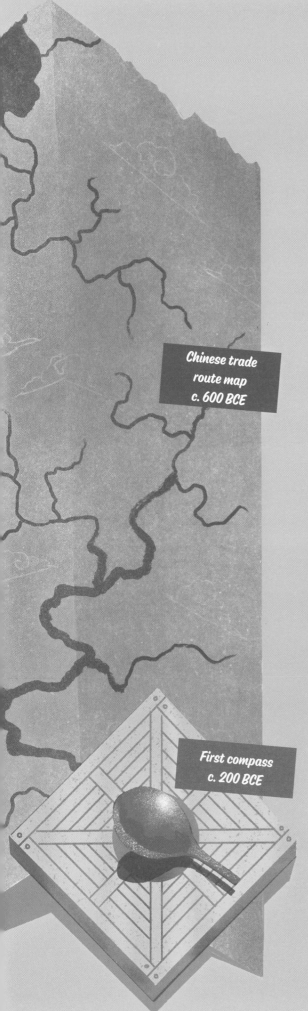

Chinese trade route map
c. 600 BCE

First compass
c. 200 BCE

To help navigate the world, we humans eventually came up with a tool to provide information on our locations and the places around us—the map. Today's maps are generally found on smartphones or the digital screens in vehicles, providing exact routes to our *destinations*. Before technology took over, paper maps were commonplace.

Show Us the Way

The oldest known surviving map is one that was carved on a unique item—a mammoth's tusk! Discovered in 1962, the map dates back to about 25,000 BCE, and it was found in a village in the Czech Republic in Central Europe. It shows landscape features like the mountains, rivers and valleys around the village.

Other early maps have been found on cave walls, including one dating back to about 15,000 BCE in the Lascaux Cave in central France. This map didn't record details of the area, however—it's a map of the stars. Experts say that what was first considered a painting of animals is actually an image of constellations, likely used to track changes in the night sky. This means these early

YOU ARE HERE

The word *map* comes from shortening the medieval Latin term *mappa mundi*. *Mappa* means "napkin," referring to the fact that medieval maps were drawn on napkins or cloth. And *mundi* is Latin for "world." So the phrase itself translates to "a napkin of the world."

This mammoth tusk was discovered during an archaeological dig. The map carved into it may have been used to help our ancestors find their way during hunting expeditions.

ZDA/WIKIMEDIA COMMONS/CC BY-SA 4.0

humans had an interest in astronomy—the study of objects outside the earth's atmosphere—long before the Babylonians and ancient Greeks, who are often thought to have been among the earliest astronomers.

Map or Myth?

The Babylonians, an ancient *civilization* that lived over 4,000 years ago, created the oldest surviving map of the world. It's scratched onto a small clay tablet about the size of your hand. The world depicted on this tablet isn't the one we know though. It's the Babylonians' idea of their world. Land is shown in the shape of a circle, with a ring of water called Bitter River surrounding it, and Babylon appears in the center of it. Beyond the circle are distant islands. And ancient text at the top of the map explains that ruined cities, gods and mythological beasts—like a giant

sea serpent and a scorpion man—live in these far-off places. Experts say this map is a combination of geographical details and Babylonian mythology rolled into one.

Put It on Paper

The ancient Greeks created the first paper maps to be used for navigation. Mapmakers of the time spent their days trying to determine the size and shape of the earth, and they were interested in charting the position of nearby territories and countries. A Greek philosopher named Anaximander is considered one of the first cartographers—that's a person who produces maps. His map showed the known lands of the time—Europe, Asia and Libya. Ancient Greeks used this map for navigation and to identify possible trade routes to nearby colonies.

Maps made by the ancient Chinese also marked out trade routes to areas

bordering China. Drawn on wooden blocks or silk, these maps were created as early as 600 BCE. Two particular maps that date from about 200 BCE were found in an ancient Chinese tomb in the 1970s. Painted on silk, they show mountains, rivers, villages and even several roads. It's believed these maps were used in a war between two kingdoms, providing information needed to attack the enemy and defend against raids.

The Places We'll Go

Maps continued to evolve as the centuries moved along, especially as people set out from here to there, discovering more

of the world. **Cartography**, or the art of making maps, became an important tool for **exploration**. This was particularly apparent once the Age of Discovery arrived. This period began in the 1400s and lasted through the 1600s. During this time many European explorers set off in their ships in search of lands new to them. They were looking to discover faster trade routes and hoping to find new goods, like precious metals and spices, to increase their wealth. European royalty often gave these explorers money for their **expeditions**, since they were looking to claim new lands as colonies in order to build their empires. These voyages led to more mapmaking, as explorers created

This map is called the Carta marina, which means "map of the sea." It is one of the earliest maps to show Nordic countries, such as Finland, Denmark and Norway. Notice the strange sea monsters in the western waters.
OLAUS MAGNUS/WIKIMEDIA COMMONS/PUBLIC DOMAIN

YOU ARE HERE

During medieval times mapmakers often drew dragons, sea monsters and other mythical creatures on map areas that were unexplored. These images were meant as a warning that danger might lurk in these unknown places.

Right This Way

Sometimes the reasons for traveling are entirely out of our hands. We have to move to stay safe.

- **War**: Throughout history, people have been forced to flee their homes as war erupts. For example, when Russia invaded Ukraine in early 2022, more than 4 million Ukrainians fled their country in the first month of the war alone, heading to such places as Poland, Romania and Hungary. And another 6.5 million people had to settle elsewhere inside their war-torn country.

- **The climate crisis**: As our planet heats up due to the climate crisis, the adverse effects go beyond higher temperatures. The climate crisis is causing flooding, droughts and shrinking sea ice, among other things. The hot and dry conditions caused by the climate crisis have also increased the risk of wildfires. In 2018 a vicious wildfire tore through the town of Paradise, California. The town was almost completely destroyed, and its nearly 30,000 residents had to move away. Fewer than 10,000 people have since returned.

- **Food shortages**: When food availability declines, people are often forced to leave their homes for somewhere with a better food supply. For instance, thousands of Central Americans from El Salvador, Guatemala and Honduras have made their way to the US border since 2020 due to food shortages, hoping to make a better life elsewhere.

YOU ARE HERE

A refugee is someone who has to leave their country to escape dangerous situations, such as war or a natural disaster, or difficult living conditions, such as a lack of food. Refugees seek safe shelter in a new place, sometimes living in temporary homes, like tents. Nearly half of the world's refugees are kids. They may escape with family, but there are those who flee alone. Some refugees will return home, however most never make it back to their homeland.

maps of their routes and the new areas they visited. These maps would then be used by other sailors to reach the same far-flung places.

While these trips linked the world together in a new way, it's important to recognize that they led to suffering for millions of Indigenous Peoples. Consider, for example, those who lived in the lands we now know as Canada and the United States. When European explorers arrived, the Indigenous Peoples had lived on this land for thousands of years. However, the Europeans made **treaties** with Indigenous communities and then broke them, using deceit to take the land for themselves. They attempted to **assimilate** the original inhabitants and force them to adopt European religions and values, even forbidding them to speak their own languages and removing children from their families. They also brought diseases that were unknown to the Indigenous Peoples, infecting millions and causing deadly epidemics. And, worse still,

millions more were murdered by these explorers who came from afar ready to claim land as their own at any cost.

TAKEN BY FORCE

After explorers arrived at what they called the New World, European settlers began to arrive in North, South and Central America, which continued the negative impact on Indigenous communities. But there were others who suffered at the hands of the European colonists as well. Many West Africans faced **forced migration**. They were sold to European ship captains as slaves and transported across the Atlantic Ocean, where they were sold to landowners. From there they were put to work on large farms and in mines where they had to dig for precious metals. While slavery had existed in ancient times, the African slave trade—which took place from the 16th to the 19th century—resulted in as many as 12 million Africans being stolen from their homelands and taken across the Atlantic to the Americas.

Tricks of the Trade

One of the tools that enabled Europeans to find their way across the vast ocean was the **compass**. The first compass was invented in China between 200 BCE and the 200s. It found its way to Europe by the 1300s, just in time for the Age of Discovery. Explorers set sail, leaving land far behind to head into the unknown, where they'd be surrounded by nothing but ocean. With a compass, they could track their location, continue along in one direction and use it to find their way back home.

Another technology that helped humans find their way more easily was the printing press. Developed by a German inventor named Johannes Gutenberg in about 1440, it meant that accurate maps could be easily produced and more widely available. One of the most influential maps was created by Belgian cartographer Gerardus Mercator. Published in 1569, his world map featured the entire surface of the earth. He didn't go on expeditions himself. Instead he gathered information from other cartographers and used his mathematical skills to show the surface of our spherical world on a flat map. This made the world easier to envision. The map became widely used by sailors navigating the world's oceans.

X DOES NOT MARK THE SPOT

While Mercator's map may be new to you, there's one type of map you've probably heard about—the pirate map. It's said to feature an *X* that marks the spot where treasure is buried. The Golden Age of Piracy spanned the years from about 1650 to 1730. During this time hundreds of pirate ships sailed the waters of the world. As you likely know, pirates weren't the friendliest folks. Famed pirates like Blackbeard and Captain Kidd spent their seafaring days attacking and robbing any ships that crossed their path. They plundered whatever items they found aboard, including food, spices, weapons, jewels and money. But you might be surprised to know they rarely buried their loot. They sold most of the stolen items once they reached a port, and they often gambled away the money they made.

So where did this legend of the treasure map come from? It likely got its start thanks to a popular 1883 novel called *Treasure Island*. Written by Robert Louis Stevenson, it tells the tale of the search for a treasure of gold hidden by an evil pirate. That said, there are those who believe there is a real pirate's treasure hidden somewhere in the Caribbean. Before he died, the pirate Blackbeard claimed he'd buried a massive treasure of gold and jewels. While people have tried their best to find this stash for the past three centuries, no one has had any luck—so far. Even though treasure maps haven't proven to be all that useful, there are many other types of maps that humans have come to rely on to get where they want to go.

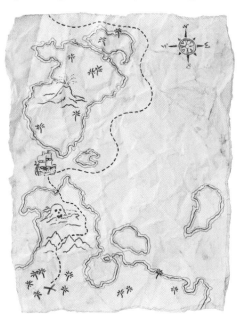

FLAMINGPUMPKIN/GETTY IMAGES

YOU ARE HERE

It's often said that educated Europeans believed the earth was flat until sometime after the 1400s. However, many historians argue this is not true. Ancient Greek scholars had determined that the planet was round as early as 600 BCE. And since Europeans studied Greek knowledge, they understood they were living on a sphere.

Right This Way

Thousands of years before the Age of Discovery, other humans found their way to North America aboard boats. In a recent study, researchers from the University of Oxford say people from Eurasia made the ocean journey about 30,000 years ago, becoming the very first humans to arrive on the continent. Another influx of people took place in about 15,000 BCE, when more travelers crossed a bridge of land and ice. Known as the Bering Land Bridge, it connected the continents of Asia and North America and was formed during the last ice age. Sea levels dropped during this era, causing the land to be exposed. That meant travelers could walk across this bridge toward North America as they followed and hunted food sources like caribou, bison and mammoths. As the ice age ended, glaciers melted, flooding the land bridge once again.

FINDING ANOTHER WAY

Maps were not the only navigational tool people used. Follow along to see how some early travelers got around:

SHARPLY_DONE/GETTY IMAGES

c. 2400 BCE

Inuit have used figures made of piled stones to help people find their way. Each structure, known as an *inuksuk*, works like a sign in the landscape, pointing the way to a good hunting spot or a place where food is stored. It may also mark a sacred place.

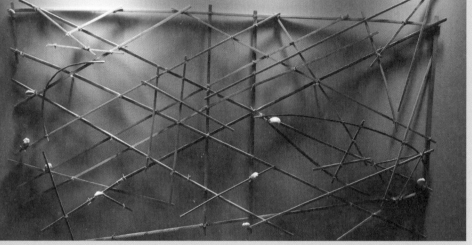

RAMA/WIKIMEDIA COMMONS/CC BY-SA 2.0 FR

c. 2000 BCE

For centuries the ancient Marshallese of the Marshall Islands in the central Pacific Ocean used stick charts made of coconut fibers and shells to navigate the sea. The tied-together coconut fibers represented specific ocean waves and currents, and the shells depicted nearby islands. It's thought these stick charts weren't carried during a journey. Instead sailors memorized charts before their voyages.

JÚLIO REIS/WIKIMEDIA COMMONS/CC BY-SA 3.0

c. 300 BCE

The ancient Romans erected columns called *milestones*, or *miliariums*, along Roman roads. These signs marked the distance between two towns. They were made of stone, and some can still be seen today along roadsides in Italy, England and Portugal.

Interactive mall maps
2015

Pocket-sized road maps
c. 1900

1900

New York City Subway map
1979

Map of the ocean floor
1957

GPS technology
1973

Three

HUMANS CHANGE COURSE

As time moved along, maps weren't just for those planning an expedition across the ocean or trying to discover a new trade route. They were relied on for much shorter trips. The mid-1700s brought about the Industrial Revolution—an era when goods began to be manufactured in factories. People from rural areas started moving to cities to look for work in the factories, and this set into motion the evolution of big cities. And *transportation* soon changed too. Before this time, most people had traveled by foot, on horseback or perhaps by boat. Soon a network of railways had been built across countries and continents, and more people began to travel for pleasure.

Riding the Rails

Trains became a common form of transportation. And map-like railway guides and travel guidebooks became popular in the 1830s, providing people with information on how to find their way. Railway guides included train schedules and snapshots of the routes that were available. Guidebooks, on the other hand,

YOU ARE HERE

While travel guidebooks were meant to give useful information to tourists, one popular book printed by a German company, called *Baedeker's Guide to Great Britain, 1937*, was put to use by German soldiers in World War II. They used the guide to identify historic buildings and monuments in England and then bombed them.

encouraged readers to travel. They focused on certain cities or countries, introducing the idea of not-to-be-missed sights, restaurants and accommodations.

The Sky Is Not the Limit

By the time the 1900s came around, humans were on the move more than ever before. Railway travel was popular, and soon cars became a go-to method of getting around. They made it especially easy to move from one place to another whenever you wanted. This meant that maps were in demand. It also meant they had to be made smaller, mostly pocket-size, so travelers could bring them along with them. Of course, maps had become more focused, providing details about cities and roads rather than continents and oceans.

Once airplanes flew onto the scene in the early 1900s, armies of pilots began to take photographs of large expanses of land from the sky. With these images, maps could be made even more detailed and accurate. Today almost all corners of the earth have been mapped, although experts say there are some remote areas, like the polar regions and spots in Central and South America, where mapping is incomplete. Drones are now the preferred tool for capturing breathtaking images of the earth from any number of angles. And they are useful for mapping. But our world changes so quickly—thanks to human activities like building roads and clearing forests, and natural occurrences like earth-quakes and shoreline erosion—that even the most recent map may not be perfect.

Look Who's Talking

One thing's for certain. With today's computer technology, it's never been easier for humans to get around. In fact,

TIME FOR A JOURNEY

Travel as a leisure activity had become more common by the late 1800s, especially among the upper-middle class. But getaways weren't an entirely new thing. In earlier times some people traveled far from home on special outings or to relax or explore.

c. 100 BCE

During the summertime wealthy Romans left cities for resort towns along the coastline of Italy, where they had vacation villas. They holidayed and entertained friends in huge homes, often with over 50 rooms, a swimming pool and large gardens, that overlooked the sea.

c. 1200–1500

Some religious Europeans set out on a long journey called a *pilgrimage*. They traveled to sacred holy sites, or shrines, where they prayed or hoped to be cured of illnesses. These pilgrims came from around the continent, including England, Portugal and France, walking for hundreds of miles over months on roads and pathways. One popular pilgrimage in Spain saw about 500,000 pilgrims visit each year during the 13th and 14th centuries.

c. 1600–1700

Upper-class young European men went on what was called the Grand Tour, traveling around Europe to learn about the art and history of such places as Rome and London. Rather than a vacation, it was considered a way for the men to complete their education. They often traveled for three or four years.

we now have maps that speak directly to us, guiding us along our routes. You may have heard them chatting away when you're on a trip in a car. *Turn left at the next stop sign.* Or: *Keep going straight for five miles* (*eight kilometers*). We've come a long way from the days of sailors having to stare up at the night sky so the stars could lead the way. Imagine what they would think of talking maps!

Chatty maps are possible due to GPS, which was developed in the 1970s. And this technology is available not only in our cars but also on airplanes, ships and even watches and smartphones. A GPS system relies on a fleet of more than 30 **satellites** that orbit the earth and constantly transmit radio signals toward the planet. Here's how

this navigation system works:

A GPS device, like your smartphone, receives radio signals from at least four of the satellites orbiting the earth. This takes less than one second.

These signals help your smartphone figure out how far it is from those satellites. With this information it can pinpoint exactly where it (and you) are located.

The GPS system in your phone then calculates where you want to go and provides you with directions.

NOW HEAR THIS

So is GPS affecting humans and our sense of direction? In a word, perhaps. According to experts like Canadian neuroscientist Véronique Bohbot, when

YOU ARE HERE

In the 1970s copies of a map were placed on board four different spacecraft heading out of our galaxy. Each map reveals the location of Earth, so that any extraterrestrials who find them can find us! These spaceships are currently still speeding into deep space. So will any of those maps help extraterrestrial life find its way to our home sweet home? We'll have to wait and see!

Right This Way

Mapmakers take their work seriously. After all, a lot of effort goes into creating an accurate map. That said, mapmakers have been known to add a little something extra to a map that's not entirely accurate. They include "paper towns"— also known as "traps" or "phantom settlements." These are places that don't actually exist. So why would a cartographer include a phony spot on their map? To catch anyone who copies the map and tries to pass it off as their own!

Funnily enough, one paper town actually ended up becoming a real place. In the 1930s two mapmakers used their initials to come up with a fake town called Agloe and added it to their map of New York State. Someone opened a shop called the Agloe General Store in the area after seeing it labeled on the map. Thanks to that, Agloe began to appear as a real town on maps of the area.

you follow the directions your GPS provides, you aren't using your hippocampus—the part of your brain that helps you make those mental maps we learned about earlier. In fact, studies show that this area of the brain essentially shuts down when we let GPS lead the way. This seems to indicate that when we frequently follow GPS directions, we're less likely to figure out our own way and create mental maps to get around. This may lead to our navigational skills becoming weaker. So, in other words, use it or lose it!

Experts say that when it comes to GPS, it's best not to depend on it too much and use it mainly in situations when directions would come in handy, like getting yourself to a new place. And even if you're using GPS, it's important to pay attention to your surroundings. Several drivers have had close calls while following their GPS's directions without being aware of the world around them, including driving into a gigantic sandpile, motoring into the ocean and nearly plunging over a cliff!

The Future of Maps

While technology has brought mapmaking a long way, the field continues to evolve. Today we're moving toward the "living" map, a type of digital map that is constantly updated in real time. It can show you what's happening on your route as you're traveling. For instance, if a road is suddenly closed due to construction or an accident, it'll show up on the map, allowing you to decide whether to stick to your route or take a detour.

Still a new technology, living maps are built by collecting data from various sources, including *radar*, videos from car dashboard cameras and images from a drone as it flies. All this data is uploaded onto an existing digital map, making it as accurate as possible. We may reach a point in the future where cameras are placed in every car or even on their roofs so that all those video systems and sensors can gather information to add to a living map. This focus on *innovation* in mapmaking is really not all that surprising though. Humans are always looking for new and better ways of doing things.

MAPS, MAPS AND MORE MAPS

While GPS is all the rage these days, that doesn't mean maps have completely disappeared.
Think about visiting an amusement park. A map often helps you find the fastest way to the ultimate coaster.
In fact, maps are still used in a number of other places:

RAWPIXEL/GETTY IMAGES

- Transit maps show the routes and stations of public transportation systems like trains, buses and ferries. Such maps help passengers easily plot their trips. Researchers have found the most complicated transit map around is the one for the New York City subway system. It has a total of 161 possible train connections.

ANDRESR/GETTY IMAGES

- When you go to the mall, a directory shows you your location and the whereabouts of all the stores and businesses in the mall. Some of today's mall maps have gone interactive, allowing you to upload them to your phone.

NASA/GODDARD SPACE FLIGHT CENTER SCIENTIFIC
VISUALIZATION STUDIO. GAIA DR2: ESA/GAIA/DPAC

- Even the night sky has maps. There are sky charts that map out the moon, stars and some of the planets that can be seen from your location. NASA has mapped out the 88 officially recognized constellations in the sky. And American research scientists recently began mapping the universe. So far they've pinpointed the location of at least 7.5 million galaxies. And they hope to catalog a total of 35 million by 2026!

NIPPON FOUNDATION-GEBCO
SEABED 2030 PROJECT

- Experts are currently working to map the ocean floor in a project called Seabed 2030. So far, only about 20 percent of the world's seafloor has been mapped. But scientists are committed to finishing the task by 2030. Of course, reaching the deepest, most out-of-the-way spots in the ocean is tricky, especially since you need vessels strong enough to withstand the water pressure at those depths. Experts are hoping a fleet of robotic vessels will help get the job done.

BIZOON/DREAMSTIME.COM

- You'll even find maps in video games. Consider *Minecraft*. You can use a map in the game to navigate around your world.

Camels
c. 4000 BCE

Horses
c. 3500 BCE

Sled dogs
c. 8000 BCE

Model T
1908

Rover safety bicycle
1885

Underground
railway system
1863

Steamships
1807

Sumerian sailboat
c. 5000 BCE

Four

THE EVOLUTION OF TRANSPORTATION

While our early ancestors had to walk or run wherever they went, we humans eventually began to look for faster ways to get around that required a lot less energy on our part. Our first solution came when we domesticated animals in Asia at least 15,000 years ago. Rather than hunting certain animals for food, we began to interact with them in a new way.

Animal Power

Eventually we tamed wild creatures and began to use them as a mode of transportation. This was a turning point in human history. The ability to move about more easily led to a stronger connection between different civilizations. It also allowed for the trading of goods. More people began migrating to new, remote places.

Can You Dig It?

While animals provided humans with a helping hand—or maybe that should be a helping hoof—people continued to find other ways to move about their environment. The first human civilizations were established alongside water, using rivers and lakes for drinking and for watering crops. But people began to recognize these waterways could be used for travel. And along came the boat. The earliest boat is thought to have been the dugout, a canoe-shaped vessel made by chopping down a tree and hollowing out its trunk. It's said to date back about 8,000 years, and it was used by ancient cultures in parts of the world including New Zealand, South America and Canada. The boats were sailed through calm water using paddles or sometimes a pole pushed along the bottom of a waterway. They were used for transporting goods and for fishing.

Setting Sail

It's believed the Sumerians—a civilization that lived in a region of the Middle East around 5000 BCE—invented the sailboat. By harnessing the wind to travel, they were able to move along two nearby rivers much faster and easier than by paddling. The sails were square and made of either a woven cloth called linen or the stems of a plant known as papyrus. By about 3000 BCE, the ancient Egyptians were using small sailboats too. These had one square sail made of cloth as well as oars for travel along the Nile River. The Egyptians used the boats for fishing and for carrying goods to trade with civilizations around the Mediterranean. As boats got bigger, more cargo could be carried, and trade with other empires became easier. The

Egyptians also used sailboats as warships by adding a bronze battering ram to them. This heavy beam could be rammed into the wooden side of an enemy boat to destroy it. And the ancient Romans got in on the warship action too. They eventually had a fleet of warships that dominated surrounding seas. They also sailed their ships around the region to protect their trading routes.

FULL STEAM AHEAD

By the 1500s sailboats played a massive role in the exploration of the globe. Explorers sailed thousands of miles, some going on voyages that took years. Soon the sailboats became larger, and more sails were added to them, meaning they could cruise faster and carry larger cargoes.

In the early 1800s the steam engine started being used to power boats. This eventually brought about boats that no longer relied on the wind at all to push them through the seas. Steamships could chart their own courses.

By the end of the 1800s, these ships had begun to carry hundreds of travelers, and some of the vessels had extravagant features like restaurants and even swimming pools. The luxury liners went on transatlantic journeys, carrying passengers looking to leave Europe behind and make new lives for themselves in the United States or Australia. Today's ocean liners cruise waters around the world. But they bring tourists on round-trip vacations rather than on one-way voyages. And, like most modern boats, they have a more state-of-the-art engine than the steam engine of the past. All this makes for a faster trip. While a steamship took about two weeks to cross the Atlantic, an ocean liner can travel the same distance in less than a week.

ALONG FOR THE RIDE

There are several creatures in the animal kingdom that have helped humans get around, including these ones:

c. 8000 BCE

Archaeologists—scientists who study ancient humans—say dogs were first used for sledding in places like Siberia, Canada and Greenland. Teams of two or more canines pulled a sled of supplies across the snowy ground, sometimes carrying items on their backs as well. A human driver would ride on the back of the sled, guiding the pack with their voice.

c. 4000 BCE

Camels were relied on in central Asia to transport goods. They were reliable creatures since they can go weeks without drinking water, even as they cross the dry desert carrying people and hundreds of pounds of supplies. Today camels are sometimes referred to as "ships of the desert." That's because they can carry loads for long distances and also because their bodies sway from side to side as they walk, sort of like a ship in rough waters.

c. 4000 BCE

Llamas were used by Indigenous people living in communities throughout South America to transport goods between the coast and the highlands. Humans led packs of llamas called *caravans* along trails through the Andes Mountains. These llama caravans made trade possible between communities. People in the lowland and coastal regions could trade fish and maize for items like wool and meat from those living in the highlands.

c. 3500 BCE

Humans began to ride horses in central Asia. Soon domesticated horses were found across the rest of Asia as well as in Europe. Horses allowed people to travel great distances quickly. And once the wheel was invented, the animals pulled wagons and carts, making it easier to haul heavy loads. They also played an important part in war. Armies of warriors rode horses to distant places to battle for and conquer the land.

YOU ARE HERE

You may have noticed that boats are named. It's thought this tradition dates back to the ancient Greeks, Egyptians and Romans, who named vessels after their gods in hopes that this would protect them as they sailed. Today boats are given all kinds of names. But choose wisely, as once you've named a boat, it's considered unlucky to change it.

Let's Roll

With boats and animals, our ancestors had a couple of ways to move about more easily. But humans set their mind on a faster way to get from here to there on land. And that's when the wheel came along. The first wheel was invented in about 3500 BCE by the Sumerians. But it took a while before the wheel began to be used for human transportation.

That began around 1500 BCE, when ancient civilizations, including the Egyptians, made horse-drawn *chariots*. But these chariots were designed with one particular thing in mind—war. They were the perfect vehicle for zipping onto battle-fields. In one of the largest chariot battles ever—the Battle of Kadesh, in 1275 BCE—the Egyptians took on an ancient people called the Hittites. Both sides rolled in with chariots—about 5,000 in total! In the end, no one won the battle and a peace treaty was declared instead.

THE WHEEL DEAL

Luckily, humans moved past the battle-field, and two-wheeled chariots started to be used for travel as well as for hauling items. And over time, we came up with a number of other ways to wheel around.

The first public buses were introduced in Paris in 1662. These horse-drawn buses ran on a schedule and had specific routes. But only the upper classes were permitted to ride them. The buses stuck around for about 15 years, until fares were increased and the nobility lost interest in climbing aboard. They disappeared, and it wasn't until about 150 years later that the next buses came along. Called omnibuses, they were passenger wagons pulled by horses. France was again first to introduce the new ride. This time everyone—both the upper and lower classes—were allowed onboard.

To reduce *congestion* on city streets, the first underground railway system opened in London, England, in January 1863. And

it was a huge success. On its opening day, 30,000 passengers tried it out. Wooden carriages pulled by steam locomotives carried passengers through the tunnel beneath the city. It took around 50 years before the rest of the system was complete. Today the London Underground—or the Tube, as it's also known—carries about two million passengers each day.

OUT FOR A SPIN

Bicycles became a big hit in the late 1800s. In the 1870s, the popular penny-farthing spun onto the scene. Its extra-large front wheel allowed the bike to move forward quickly with each pedal turn. But there was a problem with these wheeled wonders. Riders often took a "header" over the handlebars if they hit a bump or stopped too quickly. In 1885 a British inventor named John Kemp Starley changed the bike world for good when he devised a

gear system to turn bike wheels. The Rover safety bicycle had a chain and gears that turned the back wheel as the bike was pedaled. And since it was much lower to the ground, it was a safe ride.

The first affordable car came off the Ford assembly line in 1908. Called the Model T, it offered people a cheap way to get around. Millions of the cars were sold during the first decade it was available. The cars were being made so quickly because of demand that there was no time to paint them different colors. So for nearly 10 years the company sold the Model T in only one color—black.

Hit the Road

For most wheeled vehicles to get around, they need a good road system. An extensive network of roads was built during the era of the Roman Empire,

Riding a penny-farthing is a challenge. But just as challenging? Trying to get on and off the high-wheeler bicycle!

Right This Way

Sometimes even a boat can't get you there fast enough, since a pesky thing called land gets in the way. That's when you've got to get creative. In the early 1900s a canal was built through Central America to link the Atlantic and Pacific Oceans. It took a decade of work and more than 40,000 people to finish the project called the Panama Canal. But when it was complete, this new route meant ships no longer had to sail around a continent. They could simply go through it. The Panama Canal is still an important shipping route today, with about 40 vessels passing through it each day.

The city of Pompeii was once buried under ash and rock after a volcano eruption in the year 79. Today people can visit Pompeii to see its ruins, including its stone streets.
DOMAREVA.TANYA/SHUTTERSTOCK.COM

YOU ARE HERE

In 1865 the British government passed a law that required a person waving a red flag to walk in front of any car driving on the road. This law, which became known as the Red Flag Act, was meant to warn horse carriages and other road users that a car was coming and also keep the vehicle itself from being driven too quickly.

beginning around 300 BCE. The roads were created mainly to allow troops to march quickly across the empire and to connect captured cities. Roadways stretched from present-day England to northern Africa, covering 50,000 miles (80,000 kilometers). And they were well made. Crews dug trenches and filled them with soil and crushed rocks. Then the top layer was finished off with neatly arranged stone blocks.

PASS THE MESSAGE ALONG

Another road system that deserves recognition weaved its way through parts of South America in the 15th century. In fact, the Inca road system is listed as a World Heritage site, recognizing its importance and its need to be protected.

Built over a number of centuries by the Inca—a civilization that ruled the area beginning in the 1100s—the roads were designed to be used by people and pack animals, since vehicles had not yet found their way here. Soil, sand and grass were used to make the roads in many areas, while stones were laid down through the mountains. To get through the rugged land, the Inca often built bridges and stairways to complete a route. All in all, the road system covered over 25,000 miles (40,000 kilometers).

Like the Romans, the Inca built roads to help their armies find a quick route across the terrain, as well as to help with trade between communities in the highlands, jungles and along the coast. The roads were also used by a group of special runners, called the *chaski*. These fit, fast young males raced along the roads, delivering official messages throughout the empire. Since the Inca didn't have a writing system, chaskis passed along information with spoken messages. Sometimes chaskis brought more than communication. They also delivered fresh provisions, like fish and seafood, to Inca royalty.

Traveling by roads like these, which led through different types of terrain, certainly made it easier for humans to get around. But, as usual, we weren't content to stop there.

YOU ARE HERE

Most of today's highways are paved in asphalt concrete. The first modern road to be covered with the stuff was the Avenue des Champs-Élysées running through Paris, in 1824.

ROLL WITH IT

Humans have invented a number of wheeled modes of transportation besides buses, bikes and cars. Here are a few unique ones:

c. 1869

The pulled rickshaw is a two- or three-wheeled passenger cart that's hauled by a person on foot. It was invented in Japan and became a popular way to carry people through the streets of many Asian countries. By the 1930s most rickshaws had a bike attached to the front, so a person didn't have the strenuous job of pulling it along.

c. 1940s

Tuk-tuks are three-wheeled motorized vehicles that are used as taxis in places like Egypt and Thailand. They also go by the name *auto rickshaw*. These vehicles get their name from the puttering sound their small engines make.

2001

The original two-wheeled, motorized scooter called the Segway balanced itself and allowed a rider to zip around while standing up. American inventor Dean Kamen designed it as an alternative to cars on city streets. This "human transporter" got a lot of attention when it was unveiled. But less than 20 years later, the Segway still hadn't caught on and production of the vehicle shut down.

Space tourism shuttle
2021

Passenger jet
c. 1950

First person on the moon
1969

First crew on
International Space Station
2000

First airplane flight
1903

First hot-air balloon flight
1783

Five

HEADING SKYWARD

What's a human to do once they've found a way to travel on land and sea? Look up, of course. Way up. When you really start to think about it, traveling through the sky is a daunting task. But there were humans who were willing to give it a try.

The Only Way Is Up

The first expeditions into the skies began in the late 1700s. A pair of French brothers named Jacques-Étienne and Joseph-Michel Montgolfier designed a hot-air balloon. After working on the concept for a few years, the pair decided to test it by sending three animals—a rooster, duck and sheep—up into the air. They wanted to see if the high *altitude* would affect the animals. So they put the trio in a wicker cage, attached it to the hot-air balloon and sent it skyward. The balloon sailed off for about eight minutes before safely landing two miles (three kilometers) away. And all was well with the animals.

With a safe flight in the books, humans began taking to the clouds in hot-air balloons. Balloon travel could be tricky though.

YOU ARE HERE

In the late 1400s Italian artist and engineer Leonardo da Vinci sketched images of flying machines, including a helicopter-like contraption. That was 450 years before the helicopter took flight. Word is, he observed birds and studied their wings, inspiring him to consider human-powered flying machines.

Pilots had to drift with the wind, meaning they couldn't control which direction a balloon flew. Even so, ballooning was the most popular way to sail through the skies until the airplane was invented.

ALONG CAME THE AIRPLANE

In 1903 another pair of brothers took things aloft. Orville and Wilbur Wright developed the first piloted, engine-powered aircraft to fly successfully. At first the American pair tested out kites and then gliders. But on a chilly winter day in Kitty Hawk, North Carolina, they managed to fly their plane—*Wright Flyer 1*—for 12 seconds. Orville piloted this historic flight, flying 120 feet (37 meters). With more improvements over two years' time, the brothers were able to keep their plane in flight for nearly 40 minutes. This marked the start of modern aviation, or air travel.

Other inventors followed the Wright brothers, coming up with their own plane designs. Over the next two decades, newer planes able to take longer journeys were built. The first solo flight across the Atlantic Ocean took place in 1927. That's when an American pilot named Charles Lindbergh flew his aircraft—*Spirit of St. Louis*—from New York to Paris in just over 33 hours.

THAT'S BILLIONS, NOT MILLIONS

It wasn't long before air travel took off even further. In the late 1940s the first jet *airliners* appeared on the scene. They could carry about 50 passengers. By 1969 the jumbo jet had arrived. It was the largest airliner ever built and carried over 350 passengers. It helped make air travel more affordable, and millions of people took to the sky throughout the 1970s. Today the number of fliers is through the roof. According to statistics, over four billion passengers take flight during a typical year. While that's a lot of fliers, research shows that most flights are taken by a small percentage of the world's

Right This Way

With thousands of airplanes flying through the skies at any given time, it's crucial for somebody—or a whole lot of somebodies—to keep track of them so people stay safe in the sky. That's where air traffic controllers come in. These individuals monitor planes on the ground and as they're airborne, helping them safely get from place to place. Several controllers follow a plane as it flies—some monitor the plane as it takes off, others follow it on its route, and others track it when it reaches its destination.

Air traffic controllers use computer software and a radar system to keep an eye on planes and organize air traffic. They communicate with pilots using a radio, giving them flight instructions and updating them if a severe storm is in their path. No matter where they are in the world, air traffic controllers and international pilots communicate in one common language: English.

Right This Way

Humans have now set their sights on another space destination—Mars. There are currently several plans underway to reach the so-called Red Planet. China plans to send its first crewed mission to Mars in 2033. NASA is hoping for human exploration of the planet in the 2030s. And the American company SpaceX has set a lofty goal of reaching Mars by 2024.

Just how possible is this interplanetary trip? Time will tell! With our current technology, it'll take about nine months to reach Mars. And travelers will have to carry everything they need for the trip, including enough food, water, medical supplies and, of course, fuel. You do not want to run out of rocket fuel in deep space! But getting there isn't the only hurdle. Experts are figuring out how to live and survive on Mars. After all, its air is unbreathable for humans, since it has very little oxygen. And then there's the tricky exit. Researchers still have to devise a plan to help earthlings make their way back home.

This photo captures Buzz Aldrin walking on the moon. Funnily enough, astronaut Neil Armstrong is also in the image. His reflection can be seen in Aldrin's visor!

MICHAEL DUNNING/GETTY IMAGES

population. There are many frequent fliers, with some taking several flights a day. In fact, the best guess is that only about 10 percent of the world's population will hop aboard a plane each year.

And here's something to consider about these travelers who head to the skies. They aren't exactly helping out the planet by flying so much. Airplanes release greenhouse gases into the atmosphere. These gases trap the sun's heat and contribute to global warming. While there are other contributors to global warming—like cars, electricity production and factories—air travel has a major impact. So although airplanes certainly are an easy way for some of us to get around, all those flights have big consequences for the entire planet.

We Have Lift-Off

Humans have never been a species to quit while we're ahead. So, of course, once we

figured out air travel, we looked past the clouds all the way to the stars. The first human in space was Russian cosmonaut Yuri Gagarin, who headed into orbit on a spacecraft called *Vostok 1* on April 12, 1961. He circled the earth once and then ejected from his space capsule and parachuted back to solid ground. All in all, his space adventure lasted 1 hour and 48 minutes.

American astronauts traveled even farther into space when they landed on the moon in July 1969. Millions of people watched on television as three astronauts orbited the moon aboard *Apollo 11*. Then two astronauts, Neil Armstrong and Buzz Aldrin, climbed into the lunar module called *Eagle*, leaving *Apollo 11*'s command module behind. Armstrong became the first person to set foot on another world when he exited the module. Both he and Aldrin spent 2.5 hours collecting 48 pounds (22 kilograms) of soil and rock samples to bring back to Earth to be studied.

REDUCE, REUSE, RECYCLE

Space travel reached new heights in April 1981 with the launch of the space shuttle *Columbia*. It was the first spacecraft that could be used for multiple journeys. Before that time, spacecraft had generally splashed down into the sea upon returning to Earth, never to be used again. NASA's space shuttle took off like a rocket and landed like an airplane. Over the next 30 years, six space shuttles were built, and five of them blasted off on a total of 135 missions from the Kennedy Space Center in Florida. While there were many successful flights, NASA's shuttle program faced failures. One of the most devastating occurred on February 1, 2003. That's when the space shuttle *Columbia* disintegrated as it reentered Earth's atmosphere. With just minutes to go before landing, the entire crew of seven astronauts died in the accident. It's a reminder that our efforts to explore can have setbacks as well as tragic outcomes. Despite this accident, the space shuttle program continued until

the fleet was retired in 2011. Today NASA is working on new space vehicles and exploration programs with a plan to send astronauts on deep-space missions.

No Space Like Home

Once we'd figured out how to get to space, it was only fitting that we'd find a way to stay a while. That's how we ended up with the International Space Station (ISS), a large spacecraft that permanently orbits Earth and has become a home to visiting astronauts and cosmonauts. Think of it as a floating science lab in space…that weighs in at nearly 500 tons (454 metric tons)!

As you can imagine, building something in outer space is no easy feat. The ISS was built over time, and pieces were launched into space beginning in 1998. Astronauts on spacewalks put the pieces together. Two years later the first crew stayed aboard the ISS for 136 days. It took another 11 years before the space station was complete. Since then nearly

The International Space Station orbits Earth about every 90 minutes—or 16 times every 24 hours.
SCIBAK/GETTY IMAGES

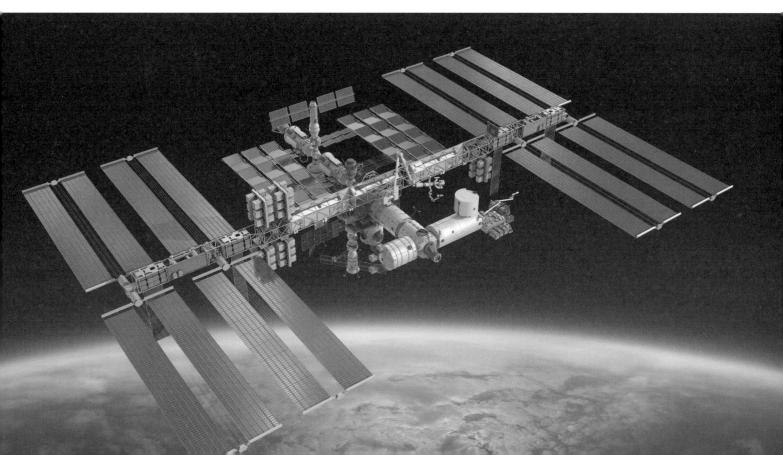

YOU ARE HERE

A spot in the Pacific Ocean has become the target for space junk plummeting back to Earth. It's named Point Nemo, and it's considered a good place to land incoming rockets and satellites since it's one of the most remote places on the planet. So far more than 250 pieces of space wreckage have crashed down into this watery spacecraft graveyard.

300 people from all over the world have visited the ISS.

SPACE GETAWAY

Until recently space travel was reserved for astronauts who'd trained long and hard for a journey into orbit. But that is slowly changing as more humans want a chance to blast off, if only for a few hours. *Space tourism* is a term used to describe space travel that's just for **leisure**. In the same way that people have hopped aboard ocean liners or airplanes to take a trip somewhere new to them, a select few are heading from here to way up there at the edge of space. That said, these space-tourism voyages don't come cheap. The price of a seat on board a spaceflight is currently starting at US$250,000—a price that's definitely out of this world.

A PRICE TO PAY

While these trips to the outer limits represent an incredible achievement for humans, it's worth considering the impact space tourism might have. For starters, there's space junk. Space junk is made up of small items that get left behind after our space missions. Experts say more than 30,000 pieces of space junk from satellites and rockets and other debris currently litter outer space. Could space-tourism journeys leave even more junk in these outer limits? While leaving garbage behind anywhere is a bad idea, space junk is also dangerous. Even the smallest piece of garbage can cause serious damage if it hits a spacecraft in orbit.

And then there's the impact space tourism may have on the environment. Rocket launches spew a variety of substances into the air. These emissions pollute Earth's atmosphere. For now the number of spaceflights is small. But with a push for more and more travel to space, this can only mean we're likely to create a bigger pollution problem.

The Only Way Is Not Up

Despite all our efforts, it may be that we don't need to head into space to discover another world. About 70 percent of the planet is covered in water, and we've yet to map out or explore most of it. While we can dive and swim about in the ocean,

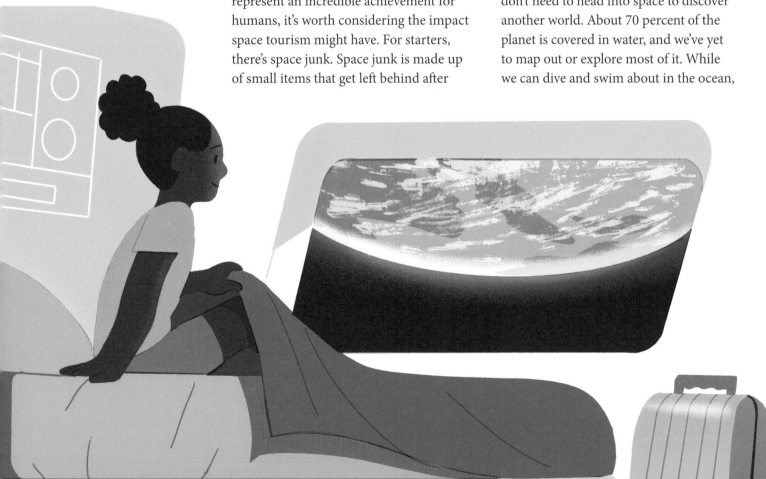

some companies are offering an entirely unique underwater experience. For instance, there are several underwater hotels that offer a room with a view…and then some! Found in places like Singapore, Dubai and Tanzania, these hotel rooms feature glass windows or walls.

There is also a fair share of underwater restaurants that offer diners a chance to eat below sea level. The Ithaa Undersea Restaurant, for example, is found deep in a lagoon off the coast of the Maldives and is surrounded by glass, allowing guests to enjoy a meal among the fish of the sea.

While hotels and restaurants may not compete with riding on a rocket, some companies are offering tourists a trip to another world—that is, a journey into the depths of the sea. The Triton DeepView is one example of an underwater luxury vehicle that's being used for sightseeing. It can carry up to 66 passengers on day trips to visit reefs and other out-of-the-way deep-sea sites. So while space tourism may be getting a lot of attention, it seems underwater tourism could be the next hottest trend in travel. And even that is only the beginning for humans and their quest for new ways to get from here to there.

YOU ARE HERE

In October 2021 a Russian actress and a film director blasted off to the International Space Station to film the first movie scenes ever shot in space. They spent 12 days in orbit before returning to Earth.

Timeline

BON VOYAGE

The first successful space-tourism trips took place within weeks of each other in the second half of 2021, allowing a few people to be launched skyward:

July 11

The VSS *Unity* spacecraft—a spaceplane—launched into suborbital space with six crew members aboard. That means the plane blasted to the edge of space, made a huge arc and glided back to Earth, not going all the way into orbit. The trip lasted over two hours, with the crew experiencing weightlessness for about five minutes before their spaceplane began its descent.

July 20

Four crew members flew into space on board the *New Shepard* rocket. Once again, the flight was suborbital. This trip lasted just over 10 minutes. The rocket descended to Earth with parachutes slowing it down, and special brakes controlled its landing.

September 15

The Crew Dragon *Resilience* capsule carried four crew members into space. The capsule flew higher than the International Space Station and went farther into space than any human has flown since astronauts last headed to the moon in 1972. The flight lasted three days before the capsule splashed down safely in the Atlantic Ocean.

Orbital Reef
c. 2030

Spaceship Neptune
c. 2025

Space elevator
c. 2050

First supersonic flight
1947

Hyperloop
c. 2030

Voyager Station hotel
c. 2027

Airbus
2035

Six

OFF TO THE FUTURE

Humans just can't help themselves when it comes to discovering new and improved ways of getting around. Designers are constantly developing new models of every type of vehicle from cars to planes to boats. Sometimes it's simply about coming up with an intriguing invention. But more often these new designs are focused on innovation—finding a better way of doing things. That can include inventing vehicles that use greener fuel to make travel more eco-friendly. Or, in the case of cars and other road vehicles, these innovations may concentrate on ways to ease congestion on our roads, which is a big problem around the world. In North America alone, the average person wastes over 50 hours a year stuck in traffic jams!

Coming Soon...Maybe

So just where are we heading when it comes to new methods of getting around in the near future? That's a tough one to know for sure. In the 1920s, people thought we'd be zipping around in flying cars by now. We all know that's not the case—although a Slovak

industrial designer named Stefan Klein recently invented a flying-car *prototype*. In the summer of 2021, his AirCar had a successful 35-minute test flight. So maybe flying cars aren't so far off. After all, the Wright brothers started with a 12-second flight in their airplane, and look how that turned out! While we can't say for sure what the future holds, there are a few predictions about what may be in store for us and how we travel.

DO YOUR THING, CAR

Let's start with cars. Besides that flying car, we've seen other innovations in recent years, including the self-driving car. These vehicles can get around on roads with little help from a human driver. The car is loaded with technology that helps it navigate, including radar, cameras, sensors and special software. At this point, cars that completely drive themselves are a no-go on our roads because the technology still hasn't made them quite safe enough.

Most of today's self-driving cars fall in the range of a Level 2 system, meaning the car can steer and accelerate, but a human must be ready to take the wheel. As for when we'll be able to sit back, relax and let the car do all the driving—that is, enjoy a Level 5 ride—experts say there's still a lot of technology to work out before a truly self-driving car hits the road. And it's suggested that could still be 30 years away.

NO MORE HUMAN ERROR?

A self-driving car is more than a cool idea. There are some real benefits to having a car take the control away from us humans. Human drivers tend to make mistakes as they drive, especially if they're distracted or tired. Of course, mistakes are perfectly natural, since we are human after all! But these mistakes can be deadly behind the wheel. In comparison, the computer on board a self-driving car is all about following the rules of the road and working together with other computers out there. So a road full of nothing but self-driving cars could help reduce the number of car accidents, possibly getting rid of them altogether. As well, their computers can map out

What will a self-driving car be able to do in the future? It may take over for a driver completely, making decisions about which route to take and tracking the driving habits of others on the road.

OLGA KURBATOVA/GETTY IMAGES

CARS RULE THE WORLD

Self-driving cars are categorized into six driving levels, from 0 to 5:

Level 0: There is no help from the vehicle whatsoever. A driver must operate it at all times.

Level 1: A driver has control at most times. The car can take over in certain instances, such as helping with parking.

Level 2: The car can accelerate and steer, but a driver must pay attention and is still in control at all times.

Level 3: A driver is like a co-pilot at this level. The car may request that the driver take over the controls. But in many cases, drivers can keep their hands off the wheel as the vehicle drives and changes lanes on mapped roadways.

Level 4: Drivers can keep their hands off the wheel and eyes off the road. The car drives and parks itself, except in severe weather.

Level 5: This level is completely driver-free. Once a passenger inputs their destination, they can sit back. There's no steering wheel or brakes inside the car.

---

routes and help traffic flow better, leading to fewer traffic jams.

That said, there's no guarantee that a self-driving car will be a perfect ride. Have you ever been working on a computer and had it crash for no apparent reason? Imagine if the computer in a self-driving car froze during a trip. That would definitely put a damper on your drive! Plus, some experts warn it may be possible for people to hack into the car's computer, making it dangerous for passengers, pedestrians and others on the road.

Make It Quick

Some designers are getting really creative when it comes to transporting people quickly between cities. Take the Hyperloop. Think of this futuristic mode of transportation as a super speedy train that travels inside a tube. The idea came about in 2013 thanks to Elon Musk, a businessperson whose companies have worked on self-driving cars and space travel. The high-speed Hyperloop system would feature floating pods that travel through a tube, carrying passengers and freight. With no wheels, these pods would move in a manner similar to the way a puck moves over an air-hockey table. But the Hyperloop would reach speeds much faster than cars, buses and most trains—possibly over 700 miles per hour (1,127 kilometers per hour)! Its tubes could be located above or below ground. The transportation system is currently being developed. Test runs, including one that carried two passengers, took place at the end of 2020 on a short Hyperloop system set up in Nevada.

Going Green

Right now airplanes are the quickest way to travel across the planet. Even so, we're still working away on innovations. For starters, designers are trying to find a way to burn less fuel during flight. That's because as an airplane burns fuel, it releases high levels of carbon dioxide into the atmosphere, which contributes to

YOU ARE HERE

The first self-driving car hit the road in 1925. That's when an American inventor tried out his driverless car on a few roads in New York City. Nicknamed the American Wonder, this vehicle was controlled by radio signals. Sort of a giant remote-controlled car, it was guided along by people in another vehicle driving behind it. Unfortunately the car hit a snag during its first-ever trip. The American Wonder ended up crashing into a car full of photographers who'd come out to snap shots of the driverless car in action! No one was seriously hurt, but that seems to have been its first and last road trip.

Is this the airplane of the future? This blended-wing airliner would not only burn less fuel but would also give passengers extra room in their seats, providing a more comfortable ride than today's planes do.
NASA/PUBLIC DOMAIN

YOU ARE HERE

The bike of the future already exists. A Japanese company recently unveiled a hoverbike, called the Xturismo, which can fly along just above the ground, using a battery-powered motor that lasts about 40 minutes. But the bike doesn't come cheap. Its price tag is US$680,000!

the climate crisis. And the airline industry's emissions continue to grow with each passing year. The best way to deal with this is by building products that are better for the environment. One example of this is the Airbus MAVERIC, which blends the wings and tail into the body of the aircraft, making it look something like a traditional kite. Its design allows it to use much less fuel than today's passenger planes. A prototype was developed in 2019, and the hope is that a version of this airliner and its "blended wing body" could carry passengers through the skies by the mid-2030s.

FAST AS YOU CAN

Supersonic flight is another advancement that could change the future of air travel. The term *supersonic* means "faster than the speed of sound." So a plane that travels at these speeds is, well, *very* fast! There have already been a few supersonic airliners in the past, including a plane called the Concorde, which could fly at twice the speed of sound. It flew passengers around the world from 1976 to 2003 and could cross the Atlantic in half the time of a typical aircraft. However, the Concorde became too expensive to run, and it was retired. Fast-forward to today. An American company named Boom is working on a supersonic plane that'll carry up to 55 passengers at a time. The company is aiming to have the aircraft in the skies by 2029. And unlike the Concorde, which had sky-high fares, Boom says its ticket prices will be affordable for most air travelers, and it will make a trip to the other side of the world just a few hours long.

Sail On

Even today's boats are getting a redesign. Remember those sailboats that helped humans travel to all corners of the world in the 1500s? A Swedish company is combining the concept of the sailboat with that of an ocean liner. The *Oceanbird* will be the largest wind-powered vessel in the world, capable of carrying over 7,000 vehicles across the sea. This sailboat/ocean-liner combo has metal rather than fabric wing sails that are similar to airplane wings. But they rotate and move up and down, helping the liner use

the wind to sail. This will make for an eco-friendly ship that can carry as much cargo as current ocean liners without burning fuel and contributing pollutants to the air. In fact, the goal is for the ship to reduce the amount of pollutants typically put into the air by today's ships by up to 90 percent. This should help offset the role these ships play in the climate crisis. Its designers say the *Oceanbird* should be ready to set sail before 2030.

YOU ARE HERE

High-speed trains are currently the fastest way to travel on land. Trains in these rail systems can hit a top speed of 370 miles per hour (595 kilometers per hour) and are found throughout Asia and Europe. If successfully developed, the Hyperloop would be nearly twice as fast. That means a traveler could get from New York to Los Angeles in about 45 minutes instead of three days.

While the Oceanbird reduces air pollution, the liner will also decrease sound pollution as it sails across the ocean without using an engine. This is good news for marine animals that rely on their hearing for navigation, communication or finding a meal.
WALLENIUS MARINE/WIKIMEDIA COMMONS/CC BY-SA 4.0

Right This Way

While we tend to sail across its surface, the depths of the ocean aren't exactly off-limits to humans. In 2019 American underwater explorer Victor Vescovo set a record for the deepest sea dive when he traveled into the Mariana Trench in the western Pacific Ocean. It's the deepest trench on the earth, and Vescovo made the trek in a submersible—a small undersea watercraft used for deep-sea research. He traveled down 35,853 feet (10,927 meters)—that's deeper than the height of Mount Everest. On an earlier oceanic dive, Vescovo discovered new sea creatures. But on this visit he spotted a few disturbing items, including a plastic bag and candy wrappers. Sadly, not only have we made it to the deepest parts of the sea, but so has our garbage.

THE GREAT BEYOND

Besides rockets and spaceplanes, other options are being considered for space tourism:

Balloon travel: A British company is working on a giant balloon that'll carry people to the edge of space for a day. The spaceship *Neptune* has a capsule beneath it with room for eight passengers and a pilot. It even has an onboard bathroom! Travelers will float up into Earth's atmosphere for a couple of hours before drifting back down to solid ground. Spaceflights are set to start before 2030.

Space elevator: Scientists are seriously considering this permanent method of transportation to space. A space elevator would see a cable or "belt" stretching from a spot on Earth to a satellite orbiting the planet. An elevator capsule would travel up and down this cable, carrying passengers or even cargo into space. And at some point in the future, an elevator might be used for travel between planets.

Space hotel: The world's first space hotel is preparing to open by the end of the 2020s. Called the Voyager Station, it's designed to resemble a Ferris wheel. While guests will be able to float around in certain parts of the structure, most of the hotel will feel like others found on Earth. To reach this hotspot, guests will have to book a trip on a spacecraft that'll dock alongside the hotel. Then they'll enter through a special access tube.

Future space station: Since the International Space Station is expected to be retired in January 2031, researchers will need a new spot to work in orbit. The Orbital Reef is a space station currently being designed by a team of companies who are partnering with NASA. Plans are for it to be in place by 2030. While the Orbital Reef will enable researchers to continue their work in orbit, its designers say it could double as a spot for space tourists to stay.

A space elevator like this one would cost billions and take decades to complete. But that doesn't mean it can't happen. In fact, researchers aboard the International Space Station have tested space-elevator technology to figure out how to make it a reality.
CHRISTIAN DARKIN/SCIENCE PHOTO LIBRARY

Conclusion

WE HAVE ARRIVED

If you've reached this point in the book, you know that humans don't fool around when it comes to getting from here to there. On horseback or in rocket ships, we'll try just about anything to make our way around the world—as well as above and below it. And we haven't even mentioned all the other methods we use to move about. Think cable cars, hang gliders, scooters, skateboards...there's no shortage of ways we humans have found to travel.

So what is it that's pushed us to move from one place to another for generation after generation? We've read about some of the reasons. Sometimes we're forced to move for our safety, whether that's because of natural disasters or war. But in other instances, we make our own choice to travel, such as deciding to migrate to another place to start a new life. Oftentimes we end up on the move simply out of curiosity. It's led generations of travelers to set off on explorations both near and far, never knowing what's around the next corner. In more recent times, it's tempted us to travel to destinations just for fun. People want to relax and unwind or have an adventure, so they set out to a particular place in the world, ready to visit and learn about this new spot.

Don't Go Anywhere

While many of us zip around the planet in any number of ways, we're also living in a time when you don't actually need to leave home to travel the world. How is that possible, you may ask? Good old technology. Take the program Google Earth. It allows you to visit the world's sights, from geographic features to landmarks, from the comfort of your house. The program can be downloaded onto your computer or smartphone. Then you're free to click away and explore the planet. Interested in visiting Egypt's pyramids? Go right ahead. What about the Amazon rainforest?

Visit away. Mount Everest base camp? No need to do all that climbing when you can simply click to it while lazing on the couch. So how does this work? Google Earth has mapped out the world by combining 3D images taken from aircraft and satellites. It's a long way from those early maps that had to be made on the spot during a trip. And this map literally puts the whole world in your hands for instant travel. Getting around has never been easier!

There's No Stopping Us

With all that being said, don't expect humans to sit at home and give up on moving about anytime soon. For one thing, we need to travel to get to places

Timeline

WEAR IT WELL

Sometimes instead of climbing aboard a vehicle to get around, we actually wear our mode of transportation:

c. 33,000 BCE

The earliest-known shoes date back to about 8000 BCE. Found in a cave in Oregon, they're a pair of sandals made of bark. However, by looking at the foot bones of ancient skeletons, experts have determined that the earliest shoes were worn over 35,000 years ago.

c. 10,000–8000 BCE

Snowshoes are designed to be worn on shoes or boots. They help distribute a person's weight so they don't sink into deep snow. Early snowshoes were made of wood and animal hide. They were likely first worn in Central Asia.

c. 1930s

The wingsuit is a special jumpsuit used by skydivers. It's designed with fabric between the legs and under the arms to help a diver extend their time in the air. So it basically lets skydivers do some hang gliding too. That said, divers do need a parachute to come in for a safe landing.

c. 1960s

A jetpack is a device worn like a backpack that allows a person to fly through the air. While the jetpack has appeared more in science-fiction books and movies than in the real world, inventors are currently working on actual versions. An Australian company recently created two jetpack prototypes that can achieve a 10-minute flight time.

like school, stores and work, and we like to visit attractions, as well as family and friends, whether they're close by or a long distance away. And then there's the fact that we're creatures who like to explore, learn and have adventures. So we're built to keep moving. Of course, some of us will stay closer to home for our entire lives. We may not have an opportunity to hop on a plane or cross the ocean to another country. And some of us will head into the outer limits. For now, that's a select few—only about 600 people out of the billions on the planet have ever made it to space. Most of us will fall somewhere between these two extremes.

One thing is certain. If history has shown us anything, it's that humans aren't afraid of the unknown. And if there's somewhere we want to go, we'll do our best to find a way to get there. The funny thing is, once we do, it's usually not too long before we're ready to get moving again. And that often means finding our way home—and right back to where we started.

Glossary

airliners—large passenger aircraft

altitude—how high something is compared to the ground or to sea level

assimilate—to absorb a person or group into a culture or society different to their own

cartography—the art of making maps

chariots—two-wheeled vehicles pulled by horses

chaskis—young male runners who were personal messengers in the Inca Empire

civilization—a large group of people who live in one area and have developed their own culture and advanced ways of living and working

compass—a tool that shows direction with the help of a moving magnetic needle that always points north

congestion—in traffic, a condition in which vehicles must move slowly because there are too many of them on the road

curiosity—the desire to learn or know something

destination—the place to which a person or an object is going

expeditions—journeys taken with specific objectives

exploration—the act of searching or examining

extinction—the state of no longer existing, such as when a species dies out and disappears from Earth

forced migration—involuntary movement of people away from their home or homeland

generation—a group of people who are born and live around the same time

Global Positioning System (GPS)—a navigation technology that uses satellites to detect the location of places on Earth

Homo sapiens—the scientific name for humankind

innovation—the creation or development of a new idea, device or way of doing something

landmarks—objects or features, like buildings or trees, that help a person find their way; also structures that are important or unique

leisure—free time

migrate—to move from one country or region to another

navigation—the process of finding your way from place to place

neuroscientists—experts who focus on understanding the workings of the brain

orbit—a circular path that one object in space takes around another one

pilgrimage—a journey, especially to a holy place

prototype—a model to test out an idea or process

radar—a system that uses radio waves to track the distance, location and speed of faraway objects

routes—specific or selected courses for traveling from one place to another

satellites—machines that orbit (go around) Earth

transportation—the means of moving people or things from one place to another

treaties—formal agreements between two parties

Resources

PRINT

Becker, Helaine. *Everything Space.* National Geographic Kids, 2015.
Bos, Samone, Phil Hunt and Andrea Mills. *Go! The Whole World of Transportation.* DK Publishing, 2006.
Chisholm, Jane. *Timelines of World History: From the Stone Age to the Millennium.* Usborne Books, 2016.
Chrisp, Peter, Joe Fullman, Susan Kennedy and Philip Parker. *History Year by Year: The History of the World from Stone Age to the Digital World.* DK Publishing, 2013.
DK Publishing. *History! The Past as You've Never Seen It Before.* DK Publishing, 2019.
Graham, Ian, and Leon Gray. *Transportation.* DK Publishing, 2012.
Graham, Ian, Andrew Nahum and Philip Wilkinson. *Firefly Encyclopedia of Transportation.* Firefly Books, 2017.

ONLINE

BBC: History for Kids: bbc.co.uk/history/forkids/index.shtml
BrainPOP Jr.: jr.brainpop.com
Britannica Kids: kids.britannica.com
DK Find Out!: dkfindout.com/us
Exploratorium: exploratorium.edu/explore
History Classroom: history.com/classroom
History for Kids: historyforkids.net
Kids Discover: online.kidsdiscover.com
Mocomi Kids: mocomi.com
NASA Kids' Club: nasa.gov/kidsclub/index.html
NASA Science Space Place: spaceplace.nasa.gov
Odyssey Online: carlos.emory.edu/htdocs/ODYSSEY/index.html
Smithsonian for Kids: si.edu/kids
Time for Kids: timeforkids.com
Wonderopolis: wonderopolis.org

Links to external resources are for personal and/or educational use only and are provided in good faith without any express or implied warranty. There is no guarantee given as to the accuracy or currency of any individual item. The author and publisher provide links as a service to readers. This does not imply any endorsement by the author or publisher of any of the content accessed through these links.

Index
*Page numbers in **bold** indicate an image caption.*

Acknowledgments

Many thanks to everyone at Orca Book Publishers, especially my editor, Kirstie Hudson, for her guidance and insight, as well as Rachel Page for her creative design work. Huge thanks to illustrator Drew Shannon for his fantastic art. And thanks to Vivian Sinclair for her thoughtful copyedits. Finally, as always, thank you to Sam and Grace, who are my North Star.

Maria Birmingham has worked in the children's publishing industry for over 25 years. She is the award-winning author of several books for young people, including *Are We Having Fun Yet? The Human Quest for a Good Time, Snooze-O-Rama: The Strange Ways That Animals Sleep* and *A Beginner's Guide to Immortality: From Alchemy to Avatars*. Maria lives in Brampton, Ontario, with her family.

Drew Shannon is an illustrator who earned a bachelor of arts at Sheridan College and has worked with many different clients including CBC, VICE Media, UNICEF, the *Washington Post* and NPR. He is the illustrator of *Extreme Battlefields: When War Meets the Forces of Nature* and *Out of the Ice: How Climate Change is Revealing the Past*. Drew lives in Toronto.

Orca TIMELINE

It's About Time!

ARE WE HAVING FUN YET?
The Human Quest for a Good Time
MARIA BIRMINGHAM

WHY HUMANS BUILD UP
The Rise of Towers, Temples and Skyscrapers
GREGOR CRAIGIE
Illustrated by KATHLEEN FU

CITIES
How Humans Live Together
MEGAN CLENDENAN
Illustrated by SUHARU OGAWA

ARE WE THERE YET?
HOW HUMANS FIND THEIR WAY
MARIA BIRMINGHAM
Illustrated by DREW SHANNON

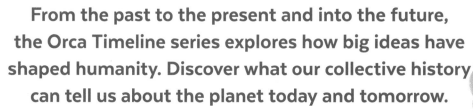

From the past to the present and into the future, the Orca Timeline series explores how big ideas have shaped humanity. Discover what our collective history can tell us about the planet today and tomorrow.

ORCA